Fly

Revised and Updated

Karen Hartley, Chris Macro, and Philip Taylor

Heinemann LIBRARY

www.heinemann.co.uk/library
Visit our website to find out more information about Heinemann Library books.

To order:
☎ Phone 44 (0) 1865 888066
🖹 Send a fax to 44 (0) 1865 314091
💻 Visit the Heinemann Bookshop at www.heinemann.co.uk/library to browse our catalogue and order online.

First published in Great Britain by Heinemann Library,
Halley Court, Jordan Hill, Oxford OX2 8EJ,
part of Harcourt Education.
Heinemann is a registered trademark of
Harcourt Education Ltd.

Editorial: Diyan Leake and Catherine Clarke
Design: Kimberly R. Miracle and
Cavedweller Studio
Illustrations: Alan Fraser at Pennant Illustration
Picture research: Melissa Allison
Production: Alison Parsons

Originated by Dot Gradations Ltd
Printed and bound in China by South China
Printing Company

ISBN 978 0 431 01980 2 (hardback)
12 11 10 09 08
10 9 8 7 6 5 4 3 2 1

ISBN 978 0 431 01986 4 (paperback)
12 11 10 09 08
10 9 8 7 6 5 4 3 2 1

British Library Cataloguing in Publication Data
Hartley, Karen, Macro, Chris and Taylor, Philip
Fly. - 2nd Edition. - (Bug Books)
595.7'7
A full catalogue record for this book is available from the British Library.

Acknowledgements
The publishers would like to thank the following for permission to reproduce photographs:
© Ardea London pp. **7** (J. L. Mason), **9** (Alan Weaving), **10** (P. Morris), **16** (Pascal Goetgheluck), **28** (Pascal Goetgheluck); © Bruce Coleman pp. **18** (Jane Burton), **20** (Felix Labhardt); © FLPA pp. **4** (B. Borell), **24**; © Heather Angel p. **17**; © Nature Photographers Ltd (Nicholas Phelps Brown) p. **23**; © NHPA pp. **11**, **12** (Stephen Dalton), **13** (Stephen Dalton), **14** (Stephen Dalton), **26** (Stephen Dalton); © Oxford Scientific Films pp. **5** (K .G. Vock), **8** (G. I. Bernard), **21** (Bob Fredrick), **22** (Andrew Plumptre), **25** (Avril Rampage), **27** (Stephen Dalton), **29** (London Scientific Films); © Photolibrary pp. **6** (Rafi Ben-Shahar), **15** (Richard Packwood), **19** (Elliot Neep).

Cover photograph of a greenbottle fly reproduced with permission of Science Photo Library (John Devries).

Every effort has been made to contact copyright holders of any material reproduced in this book. Any omissions will be rectified in subsequent printings if notice is given to the publishers.

Contents

Some words are shown in bold, **like this**. You can find out what they mean by looking in the glossary.

What are flies?

housefly

Flies are **insects**. There are many different types of fly. The flies we see most are houseflies and bluebottles.

4

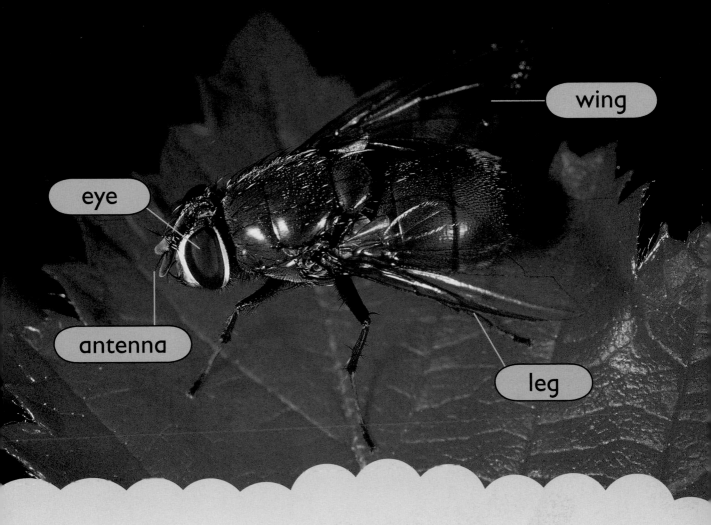

wing

eye

antenna

leg

Flies have six legs and two wings. Their eyes are very big. They have two **antennae** that they use for smelling.

5

What do flies look like?

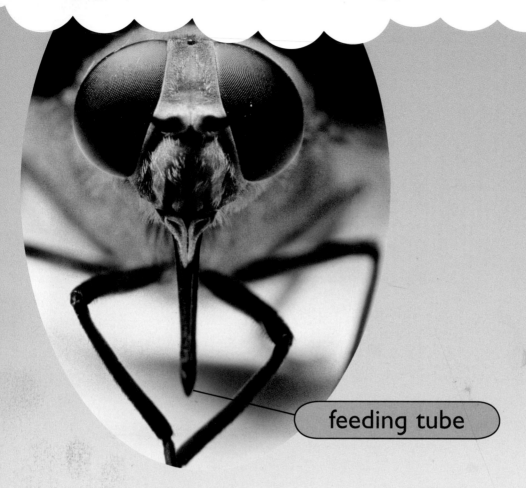

feeding tube

A fly does not have a mouth or teeth.
It eats through a long tube at the front
of its head. Flies have little holes in their
bodies for breathing.

6

Flies can be lots of different colours.
Bluebottle and greenbottle flies
are shiny. This hover fly has bright
yellow stripes.

How big are flies?

Some flies are very small. The midge in this photo is not much bigger than the full stop at the end of this line.

8

Houseflies and bluebottles are fat and hairy. Crane flies are long and thin. This fly is called a robber fly. It can be as long as a man's finger!

How are flies born?

egg

Houseflies and bluebottles lay hundreds of eggs. They lay them in rotting vegetables or in bad meat. Sometimes flies lay eggs in our food.

10

maggot

egg

After about two days the eggs **hatch** into **larvae**. The larvae of bluebottles and houseflies are called maggots. The maggots wriggle around and look for food.

How do flies grow?

pupa

The maggots grow quickly and get too big for their skins. The old skin falls off and they grow a new one. This is called **moulting**. After about ten days, the maggot turns into a hard case called a **pupa**.

12

Inside the pupa, the maggot changes into a fly. After about six days, the **adult** housefly crawls out of the hard pupa case.

pupa case

adult fly

How do flies move?

Flies move very quickly through the air. Their wings make a buzzing sound as they fly.

14

Some very small flies move around in a big group. This is called **swarming**.
A swarm can look like a cloud.

What do flies eat?

Male bluebottles and houseflies suck up **nectar** from flowers. The **females** sometimes come into our kitchens and nibble our food.

Flies squirt juice onto their food. This
makes the food go soft. The fly then
sucks the food through its feeding tube.
Some tiny flies suck blood from animals.

17

Which animals eat flies?

spider

insect

web

Spiders like to eat flies. They catch flies
and other insects in their sticky webs.
Birds and frogs also eat flies.

Many animals eat the **larvae** of flies. Fish eat larvae that live near rivers and lakes. Many birds like to eat maggots.

Where do flies live?

Flies live in most parts of the world.

Some flies live in shady places near water.

Others live near plants, fruit, and flowers.

These flies live on animal **droppings**.

20

Many **adult** flies live near rotting food and rubbish. The **larvae** can live underground or under the **bark** of trees.

How long do flies live?

pupa

adult fly

The housefly lives for about 21 days after it comes out of its **pupa** case. Most flies die when the weather gets cold, but some flies sleep through the winter.

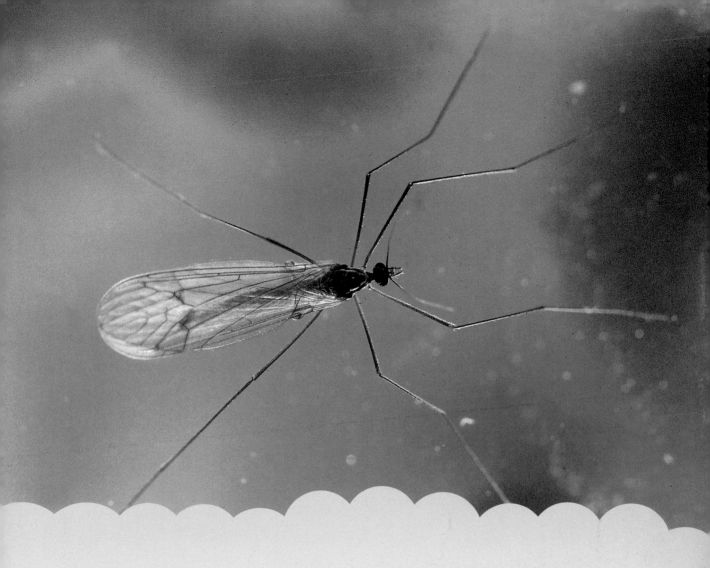

Some **adult** midges live only for one day. This is just long enough for the **female** to **mate** and lay her eggs.

23

What do flies do?

Houseflies and bluebottles spend most of their time looking for food. The **females** often come into our houses.

Many flies are **pests**. They pick up **germs** from dirty places. The flies bring the dirt and germs into our houses and onto our food.

How are flies special?

Flies have sticky pads on their feet. The pads help them walk up windows. They can even walk upside down.

26

Flies have very special eyes. They are made of thousands of small parts. Each part sends a different picture to the fly's brain.

eye

Thinking about flies

Here is a picture of a fly on some food.
What will the fly do to the food so it can
suck it up easily?

These housefly's eggs have just been laid. How long will it be before they **hatch** into **larvae**?

Bug map

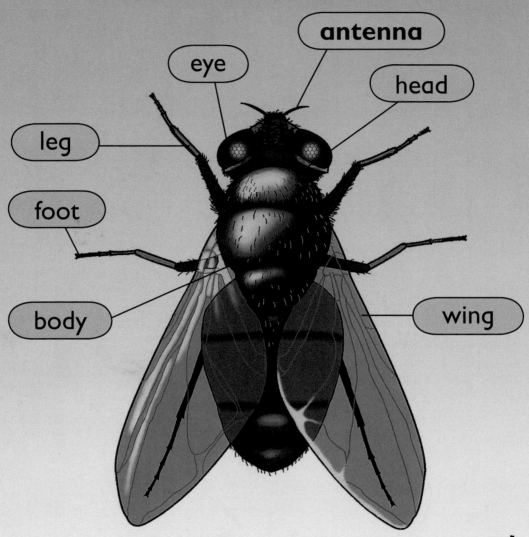

antenna

eye

head

leg

foot

body

wing

Actual size

30

Glossary

adult grown-up

antenna (more than one = antennae) thin tube that sticks out from the head of an insect. Antennae can be used to smell, feel, hear, or sense direction.

bark hard skin around a tree

droppings body waste from an animal

female animal that can lay eggs or give birth to young

germ tiny living thing that can get inside your body and make you ill

hatch to break out of an egg

insect small animal with six legs and a body with three parts

larva (more than one = larvae) baby insect that hatches from an egg. It does not look like the adult insect.

male animal that can mate with a female to produce young

mate when a male and female come together to make babies

moulting time in an insect's life when it gets too big for its skin. The old skin drops off and a new skin is underneath.

nectar the sweet juice found inside flowers

pest an animal that causes damage or hurts other animals

pupa (more than one = pupae) larva with a hard case around its body before it turns into an adult

swarming when lots of insects fly very close to each other

31

Index

More books to read

First Library of Knowledge: World of Bugs, Nicholas Harris (Blackbirch Press, 2006)

Minibeasts: Going on a Bug Hunt, Stewart Ross and Jim Pipe (Franklin Watts, 2006)

My First Book of Bugs and Spiders, Dee Phillips (Tick Tock Media, 2005)